Brutalist Plants

Hoxton Mini Press *is a small indie publisher
based in east London. Our small office
overlooks a canal – a reminder of how
much nature courses through this concrete
jungle. We make artistic books that are both
beautiful and accessible and aim to remind
readers of the richness of urban life.*

OLIVIA BROOME

Brutalist Plants

HOXTON MINI PRESS

Bucharest, Romania

Greening the Grey

ALICE FINNEY

In its five-decade history, the Barbican has gone by many names. What resonates most with me, when looking at it through the lens of Olivia Broome's *@brutalistplants* Instagram account, is prolific British architecture and design critic Oliver Wainwright's description of the estate as a 'Brutalist hanging gardens of Babylon'. As is the case with every photograph in this carefully curated collection, raw concrete tiers collide with verdant greenery, shining a light on the curious and oft-overlooked intersection between nature and Brutalist architecture.

Many of these refreshingly diverse photographs have been shot in Western Europe, where Brutalism originates. The term Brutalism derives from the French *Béton brut*, which translates as 'raw concrete'. It was coined by Le Corbusier to describe his Unité d'Habitation in Marseille, France, and then popularised by the architectural historian Reyner Banham in 1955 when writing about Brutalism in Britain. In the shadow of World War II, Brutalism was often seen as an antidote to the decorative styles preceding the movement, and a framework for delivering the radical change needed to regenerate cities across the continent.

By the 1960s and 1970s, the raw concrete movement had spread from Europe to much warmer climes around the globe. Over 156 photographs, Broome takes us on a world tour of these buildings, capturing the manifold ways in which sprawling shrubbery, trailing trellises and great woodland trees – able to cast entire tower blocks in shadow – converge with imposing forms and monolithic grey facades. In the forests of Mexico, a tropical landscape serves as the dramatic counterpoint to ashy-hued, urban forms (p.10). In Quezon City, palms and grasses sprout and flex in internal courtyards, inspiring us to reimagine our

The National Theatre, London, United Kingdom. *Architect: Denys Lasdun*

understanding of how we relate to the natural world (p.130). But, above all, it is in the most unexpected of places – think sunken lightwells, arid landscapes or abandoned, decaying industrial sites – that the marriage of concrete and rich plant life is most remarkable. It is in that liminal space – between rotting stone steps, where moss hides and life seems almost impossible – that we begin to understand the truly indomitable power of nature.

Brutalism has undergone something of a revival in recent years. Garnering the respect and admiration of a new generation of aficionados using social media as a platform to share their knowledge, images of renovated concrete bunkers, sculptural office blocks and residential skyscrapers are shared and emulated. What's most exciting, though, is that this new cohort of Brutalism lovers seek to go beyond the aesthetic preoccupation with the movement and, spurred on by the environmental crisis, address how these heritage buildings might be future-proofed by way of adaptive reuse and renovation. Instagram, Reddit and TikTok have become Petri dishes for the cultivation of nature and buildings, and serve as fertile ground for new concepts, such as the viral hashtag #ecobrutalism – loosely defined as a modern hybrid architectural style that combines traditional man-made reinforced concrete buildings with the natural world. Its popularity reflects the growing appetite for buildings that are constructed with consideration for our planet.

In this context, Broome's *Brutalist Plants* taps into the zeitgeist, encouraging readers to adopt a new perspective that goes beyond the concrete – in a nuanced fashion. As an ecological snapshot across geographies and time zones, it addresses how nature elevates existing Brutalist structures to the status of modern wonder, creating myriad Brutalist hanging gardens of Babylon.

Sourced from hundreds of professional and emerging photographers around the world, this is the first time these images have been brought together in a book. Viewed side by side, they form a compelling visual compendium that reminds us that architecture is not solely about bricks and mortar. Our built environment is a statement about humanity, which is made infinitely more vibrant when intertwined with nature.

Grey Area, Batangas, Philippines.
Architect: Cali Architects

The story of Brutalist Plants

OLIVIA BROOME

All palaces are temporary palaces. Since reading these words on a light installation by artist and poet Robert Montgomery, they have rung true for many aspects of my life and the way I have made peace with change. A relationship, a childhood home, a state of stability, a space you might never walk into again: these are all temporary palaces.

Brutalism is composed of layers, surfaces, mezzanines, patterns. Some structures are ziggurats, some curvilinear. Whether erected to commemorate battles or as a rushed attempt to house a growing urban population, these concrete palaces command attention. Brutalist architecture is loyal, unwavering, stoic: the ultimate shelter. Imposing in all the right-angled ways and reassuringly familiar to the post-Corbusier generation in Europe. My upbringing in Switzerland, with its enduring Brutalist heritage, certainly cemented my love for it.

Throw in a gravity-defying shrub, a reaching evergreen, some fanned foliage, and the harshness of *béton brut* is instantly softened: reminded that its home is our green planet, its purpose to serve society. Plants offer a counterpoint, grounded in the silt and earth from which these forceful structures were built. How can anyone say no to the pleasing perforations of a Monstera leaf?

Brutalist Plants started as an Instagram account in 2018, sparked by an interest in curating images I could not find collected elsewhere. Jutting grey angles meet wily green fronds – their appeal and contrast fascinated me. Dystopian buildings set against nature, with little human presence to be seen. The world stands still – the snapshots seem timeless. Is this the end of the world? Or a fresh new build waiting to be furnished?

Bringing together these images has done more than satisfy my aesthetic needs. It has unexpectedly and delightfully built a small community of 'Brutalist plant' enthusiasts: architects, urban explorers, horticulturalists and creatives. This book is a collaboration with photographers and *@brutalistplants* Instagram followers. Without their kind permission in allowing me to repost their photography over the years, I would have had little to work with. I am grateful to each person involved for capturing the diversity of this architectural movement and the flora that completes it.

Time passes and styles go in and out of fashion. Brutalism is no exception. These powerful palaces are ever-oscillating between being listed and being demolished. This is even more reason to honour these debated 'monstrosities' before they are reduced to rubble or, better yet, abandoned to the mercy of creeping vines through concrete cracks...

Everything is temporary; make the most of all your palaces.

Olivia Broome is the creator and curator behind @brutalistplants – the Instagram account which has grown into a community of photographers and fans of all things nature and concrete. She grew up in Geneva, Switzerland, and now lives in London, unironically surrounded by houseplants and concrete.

(Above) Casa Alférez, Cañada De Alferes, Mexico. *Architect: Ludwig Godefroy*
(Opposite) La Vallée, Basse-Normandie, France. *Artwork by Karsten Födinger*

(Above) House in Vuissens, Switzerland. *Architect: Deschenaux Architects*
(Opposite) Casa Entreparotas, Colima, Mexico. *Architect: Di Frenna Arquitectos*

(Previous) Reinforced hillside, Aogashima, Tokyo, Japan
(Above) Unité d'Habitation, Marseille, France. *Architect: Le Corbusier*

Morland Mixité Capitale, Paris, France. *Architect: David Chipperfield Architects*

Spomenik na Korčanici, Bojište, Bosnia and
Herzegovina. *Architect: Ljubomir Denković*

(Above) Lunder Center at Stone Hill, The Clark, Williamstown, MA, United States. *Architect: Tadao Ando*
(Opposite) Casa Monterrey, Monterrey, Mexico. *Architect: Tadao Ando*

(Previous) Cholula, Mexico. *Architect: Dellekamp Arquitectos*
(Above) La Maison Radieuse, Rezé, France. *Architect: Le Corbusier*

Water tower, Clamart, France

(Above) Monument honouring the 40th anniversary of the liberation of Pinsk ('Three bayonets'), Pinsk, Belarus
(Opposite) Monument to the Revolution, Kozara National Park, Prijedor,
Bosnia and Herzegovina. *Architect: Dušan Džamonja*

Water towers, Sausset Parc, Aulnay-sous-Bois, France

(Above) Mošćenička Draga, Croatia
(Overleaf) Hotel Podgorica, Podgorica, Montenegro. *Architect: Svetlana Kana Radević*

Monument to the Fighters Fallen in the People's Liberation Struggle,
Ilirska Bistrica, Slovenia. *Architect: Živa Baraga and Janez Lenassi*

Hoyerswerda, Germany

(Above) I-Resort, Nha Trang, Khanh Hoa, Vietnam. *Architect: A21 Studio*
(Opposite) V2 House, Nghi Loc, Nghe An, Vietnam. *Architect: TNT Architects*

Geisel Library, UC San Diego, San Diego, CA, United States. *Architect: William Pereira*

(Opposite) Heiligkreuzkirche (Holy Cross Church), Chur, Switzerland. *Architect: Walter Maria Förderer*
(Above) University of St. Gallen, St. Gallen, Switzerland. *Architect: Förderer Otto Zwimpfer*

BUSINESS OFFICE
2nd FLOOR
Printing · Advertising
Subscription · Payment

オフィスは二階
印刷・広告・購読・支払い

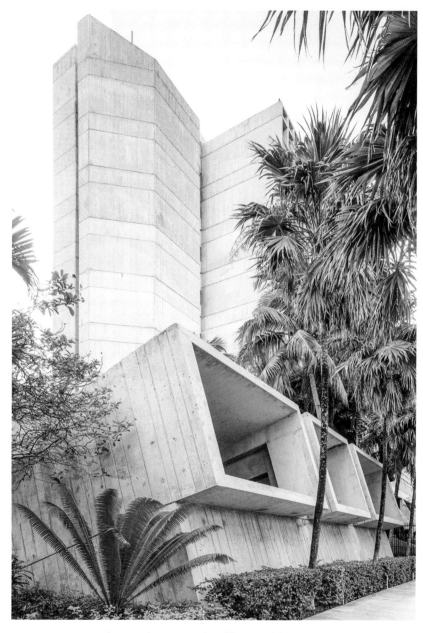

(Opposite) Hawai'i Hochi Building, Honolulu, Hawaii. *Architect: Kenzō Tange*
(Above) Mailman Center for Child Development, University of Miami,
Miami, FL, United States. *Architect: Hilario Candela*

National Gallery of Australia, Kamberri/
Canberra, Australia. *Architect: Col Madigan*

(Above) Alexandra & Ainsworth Estate, London, United Kingdom. *Architect: Neave Brown*
(Opposite) Bridge in Hong Kong

Llyn Celyn Reservoir,
Gwynedd, Wales

(Previous) London, United Kingdom
(Opposite) Cool House, Bharuch, India. *Architect: Samira Rathod Design Atelier*

Planter Box House, Kuala Lumpur, Malaysia. *Architect: Formzero*

Shaughnessy Place, Vancouver, Canada. *Architect: Blair Macdonald (McCarter Nairne and Partners)*

Opera House, Burgas, Bulgaria

Parc Floral de Paris, Paris, France

(Opposite) Hotel Dobrudja, Albena, Bulgaria. *Architect: Roy F. France*
(Above) Les Choux, Créteil, France. *Architect: Gérard Grandval*

PARKROYAL on Pickering, Singapore.
Architect: WOHA

Asoke Tower, Bangkok, Thailand

(Opposite and above) Bangkok, Thailand

Moss growing on a wall, unknown location

Cameron Offices, Belconnen, Canberra, Australia. *Architect: John Andrews*

(Previous) Monument to the Fallen Soldiers of the Kosmaj Detachment, Kosmaj Mountain Park, Serbia. *Architect: Gradimir Medaković and Vojin Stojić*
(Opposite) Planter Box House, Kuala Lumpur, Malaysia. *Architect: Formzero*

(Above) L House, Valle de Bravo, Mexico. *Architect: Dellekamp Arquitectos*
(Opposite) Abandoned building, Philippines

(Above) Macau, China
(Opposite) South-Kendall Campus, Miami Dade College, Miami, FL, United
States. *Architects: Ferendino Grafton Skeels Candela Pancoast*

(Opposite) Bosco Verticale, Milan, Italy. *Architect: Stefano Boeri*
(Above) Chempenai House, Kuala Lumpur, Malaysia. *Architect: WHBC Architects*
(Overleaf) Jewish Museum Berlin, Garden of Exile, Berlin, Germany. *Architect: Daniel Libeskind*

(Previous) Kraggenburg, The Netherlands
(Above) Orlické hory, Czechia

(Above) The Seawall, Blackpool, United Kingdom
(Overleaf) Concrete sea defences, Felixstowe, Suffolk, United Kingdom

(Opposite) La Tulipe, Geneva, Switzerland. *Architect: Jack Vicajee Bertoli*
(Above) Roberto Garza Sada Centre, University of Monterrey, Monterrey, Mexico. *Architect: Tadao Ando*

Extension of the Museum of Fine Arts, Caracas, Venezuela.
Architect: Carlos Raúl Villanueva and Oscar Carmona

Pillars, Hong Kong

Coong's Garden House, Vinh City, Vietnam. *Architect: Nguyen Khac Phuoc Architects*

Namly House, Singapore.
Architect: CHANG Architects

(Opposite) Barbican Estate, London, United Kingdom. *Architect: Chamberlin, Powell and Bon*
(Overleaf) Former Yugoslav Memorial Home and Political School, Kumrovec Croatia

(Opposite) Palm Greenhouse, Botanic Garden, Jagiellonian University, Kraków Old Town, Poland
(Above) Jurong Bird Park, Jurong, Singapore. *Architect: John Yealland and J. Toovey*

(Above) Velletri House, Cranbrook Estate, London, United Kingdom. *Architect: Skinner, Bailey, Lubetkin*
(Opposite) Broadwater Farm Estate, London, United Kingdom. *Architect: C.E Jacob and Alan Weitzel*

Habitat 67, Montreal, Canada. *Architect: Moshe Safdie*

Aragua government building, Maracay, Venezuela. *Architect: José Puig*

(Above) Église Saint-Jacques, Montrouge, France. *Architect: Éric Bagge*
(Overleaf) Cape Schanck House, Melbourne, Victoria, Australia. *Architect: Paul Morgan Architects*

(Opposite) Concorde Condominium and Office Building, Legaspi Village, Makati City, Philippines. *Architect: Cresenciano De Castro*
(Above) State University dormitories, Tbilisi, Georgia.
Architect: Sh. Kachkachishvili, E. Kopaladze, B. Maminaishvili, et al.

Hotel Igman, Sarajevo, Bosnia and Herzegovina. *Architect: Ahmed Džuvić*

(Previous) Memorial Complex to the Battle of Sutjeska, Sutjeska National Park,
Bosnia and Herzegovina. *Architect: Sakeb Hadzihalilovic*
(Above) Verdant facade, unknown location
(Opposite) Edificio Planeta, Barcelona, Spain. *Architect: Enric Tous & Josep Maria Fargas*

(Previous) Mill Owners' Association Building, Ahmedabad, Gujarat, India. *Architect: Le Corbusier*
(Opposite) White Walls Tower, Nicosia, Cyprus. *Architect: Atelier Jean Nouvel*

(Previous) Bosco Verticale, Milan, Italy. *Architect: Stefano Boeri*
(Above) Flamatt 1, Flamatt, Switzerland. *Architect: Atelier 5*

Evangelische Friedenskirche (Peace Church), Monheim-Baumberg, Germany. *Architect: Walter Maria Förderer*

Wright College, Chicago, IL, United States.
Architect: Bertrand Goldberg

(Opposite) Borderless House, Kuala Lumpur, Malaysia. *Architect: Formzero*
(Overleaf) Calouste Gulbenkian Museum, Lisbon, Portugal

Apartment in Untergiesing-Harlaching, Munich, Germany

(Above) Philippine Social Science Center, Quezon City, Philippines
(Opposite) Villa KD45 Residence, Ghaziabad, India. *Architect: Studio Symbiosis*

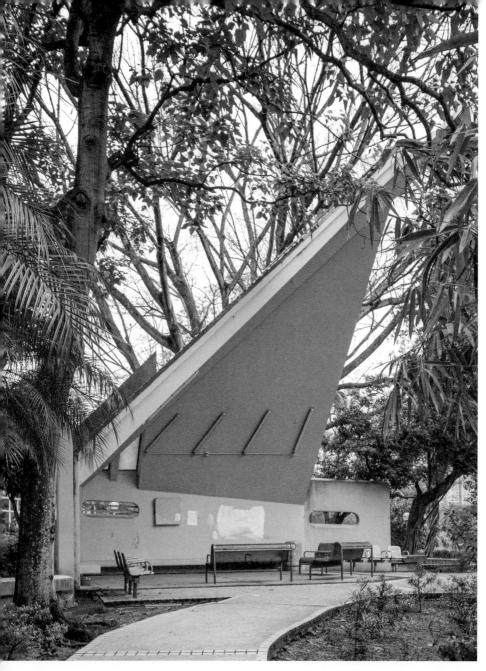

Kwong Fuk Estate, Tai Po, Hong Kong

House of Concrete Experiments, Alibag, India. *Architect: Samira Rathod Design Atelier*

(Above) UN Park Apartments, Lima, Peru. *Architect: Barclay and Crousse*
(Opposite and overleaf) Krung Thai Bank, Bangkok, Thailand. *Architect: Amorn Sriwong*

Mill Owners' Association Building, Ahmedabad, Gujarat, India. *Architect: Le Corbusier*

(Opposite) The Evergreen Building, Vancouver, Canada. *Architect: Arthur Erickson*
(Above) Barbican Estate, London, United Kingdom. *Architect: Chamberlin, Powell and Bon*

(Previous) Kadinjača Memorial Complex, Užice, Serbia. *Architect: Miodrag Živković and Aleksandar Dokić*
(Above) Bayer Schering Building, Berlin, Germany. *Architect: Kiemle, Kreidt & Partner*

Marseille, France

(Opposite) Simon Fraser University, Burnaby, Canada. *Architect: Arthur Erickson*
(Overleaf) The Interlace, Singapore. *Architect: OMA, Ole Scheeren*

Bridge near Ramkhamhaeng University, Bangkok, Thailand

The University of British Columbia, Vancouver, Canada. *Architect: Arthur Erickson*

Casa de Vidro, São Paulo, Brazil. *Architect: Lina Bo Bardi*

926 Craftsman Museum, Hangzhou, China. *Architect: TJAD Original Design Studio*

(Above) Bali, Indonesia. *Architect: Patisandhika and designer Dan Mitchell*
(Opposite) Casa Paulo Mendez da Rocha, São Paulo, Brazil. *Architect: Paulo Mendes da Rocha*

(Above) Mailman Center for Child Development, University of Miami, Miami, FL, United States. *Architect: Ferendino Grafton Spillis Candela*
(Opposite) Ruined building in the former Republic of Pavlov, Lithuania

(Previous) Abandoned bunkers, Borsh, Sarandë district, Albania
(Opposite) Praxis Home (Casa Hernández), Mexico City, Mexico. *Architect: Agustín Hernández Navarro*

(Opposite) Casa Cubo, São Paulo, Brazil. *Architect: Studio MK27*
(Above) Calouste Gulbenkian Museum, Lisbon, Portugal

(Previous) Geisel Library at UC San Diego, San Diego, CA, United States. *Architect: William Pereira*
(Above) Kapelusz (The Hat), Exhibition Hall, Chorzów, Poland. *Architect: Jerzy Gottfried*
(Opposite) Sound mirrors, Kent, United Kingdom
(Overleaf) Monument to the Revolution, Korčanica Memorial Zone, Grmeč, Bosnia.
Architect: Ljubomir Denković with Milovan Matović & Savo Subotin

Memorial Complex to the Battle of Sutjeska, Sutjeska National Park,
Bosnia and Herzegovina. *Architect: Sakeb Hadzihalilovic*

(Previous) Zen Spaces Residence, Jaipur, Rajasthan, India. *Architect: Sanjay Puri Architects*
(Above) Maison du Brésil, Paris, France. *Architect: Le Corbusier*

The University of Manchester, Manchester, United Kingdom

(Above) Dunelm House, Durham University, Durham, United Kingdom. *Architect: Richard Raines*
(Opposite) Alexandra & Ainsworth Estate, London, United Kingdom. *Architect: Neave Brown*
(Overleaf) Les Étoiles d'Ivry, Paris, France. *Architect: Jean Renaudie*

(Opposite) Wolff House, Los Angeles, CA, United States. *Architect: John Lautner*
(Above) Planter Box House, Kuala Lumpur, Malaysia. *Architect: Formzero*

(Above) Borderless House, Kuala Lumpur, Malaysia. *Architect: Formzero*
(Opposite) Casa Monterrey, Monterrey, Mexico. *Architect: Tadao Ando*

(Previous) Cornwall Gardens House, Singapore. *Architect: CHANG Architects*
(Above) Asahi Beer Oyamazaki Villa Museum of Art, Kyoto, Japan. *Architect: Tadao Ando*
(Opposite) L House, Valle de Bravo, Mexico. *Architect: Dellekamp Arquitectos*

(Opposite) Torres Blancas, Madrid, Spain. *Architect: Francisco Javier Sáenz de Oíza*
(Above) 345 Meatpacking, New York City, NY, United States. *Architect: HTO and Future Green Studio*

926 Craftsman Museum, Hangzhou, China.
Architect: TJAD Original Design Studio

926 Craftsman Museum, Hangzhou, China.
Architect: TJAD Original Design Studio

(Opposite) Ministry of Transportation, Tbilisi, Georgia. *Architect: George Chakhava and Zurab Jalaghania*
(Above) UFO Observation Deck, Bratislava, Slovakia. *Architect: J. Lacko, A. Tesár*

Les Étoiles d'Ivry, Paris, France. *Architect: Jean Renaudie*

Hotel building after the 2004 tsunami, Phuket, Thailand

(Opposite) South-Kendall Campus, Miami Dade College, Miami, FL, United States.
Architect: Ferendino Grafton Skeels Candela Pancoast
(Above) Harding Boutique Hotel, Ahangama, Sri Lanka. *Architect: ANARCHITECT*

(Above) The National Theatre, London, United Kingdom. *Architect: Denys Lasdun*
(Opposite) The Barbican Conservatory, London, United Kingdom. *Architect: Chamberlin, Powell and Bon*
(Overleaf) The abandoned Haludovo Palace Hotel, Krk Island, Croatia. *Architect: Boris Magaš*

Image credits

Brutalist Plants
First edition, second printing

This edition printed 2024
First published in 2024 by Hoxton Mini Press
Copyright © Hoxton Mini Press 2024.
All rights reserved.

Text by Olivia Broome
Editing by Zoë Jellicoe
Production design by Richard Mason
Proofreading by Florence Ward
Editorial support by Leona Crawford

ISBN: 978-1-914314-48-3

Printed and bound by Livonia Print, Latvia

Hoxton Mini Press is an environmentally conscious
publisher, committed to offsetting our carbon footprint.
This book is 100 per cent carbon compensated, with
offset purchased from the printer's offsetting scheme.

Every time you order from our website, we plant a tree:
www.hoxtonminipress.com

Back cover photographs:

(Top left) Namly House, Singapore.
Architect: CHANG Architects © Albert Lim KS

(Top right) Bucharest, Romania
© Bogdan Anghel - @bogdananghel

(Bottom left) Evangelische Friedenskirche
(Peace Church), Monheim-Baumberg, Germany.
Architect: Walter Maria Förderer
© Bildarchiv Monheim GmbH / Alamy Stock Photo

(Bottom right) Harding Boutique Hotel, Ahangama,
Sri Lanka. *Architect: ANARCHITECT © Paul Harding*
@hardingboutiquehotels @anarchitect_co

MIX
Paper | Supporting
responsible forestry
FSC
www.fsc.org   FSC® C002795